The Forgotten
Victims of
the Holocaust

Titles in *The Holocaust in History Series*

**Crimes and Criminals
of the Holocaust**
0-7660-1995-0

**Impact of
the Holocaust**
0-7660-1996-9

**The Forgotten Victims
of the Holocaust**
0-7660-1993-4

**The Jewish Victims
of the Holocaust**
0-7660-1992-6

**Hitler's Rise
to Power
and the Holocaust**
0-7660-1991-8

**Resisters and Rescuers—
Standing up Against the
Holocaust**
0-7660-1994-2

–The Holocaust in History–

The Forgotten Victims of the Holocaust

Linda Jacobs Altman

Enslow Publishers, Inc.

40 Industrial Road   PO Box 38
Box 398   Aldershot
Berkeley Heights, NJ 07922   Hants GU12 6BP
USA   UK

http://www.enslow.com

J
940.53
ALT

Library of Congress Cataloging-in-Publication Data

Altman, Linda Jacobs, 1943-
    The forgotten victims of the Holocaust / Linda Jacobs Altman.
      v. cm. — (The Holocaust in history)
    Includes bibliographical references and index.
    Contents: Building the "Master Race" — The Polish victims — The Russian
Campaign — The Gypsies of Europe — The race criminals.
    ISBN 0-7660-1993-4
    1. World War, 1939-1945—Atrocities—Juvenile literature. 2. Genocide—
Juvenile literature. 3. War crimes—Juvenile literature. 4. Romanies—Nazi
persecution—Juvenile literature. 5. Gays—Nazi persecution—Juvenile literature. 6. World War, 1939-1945—Europe, Eastern—Juvenile literature. [1. World
War, 1939-1945—Atrocities—Juvenile literature. 2. Genocide—Juvenile literature—Juvenile literature. 3. Romanies—Nazi persecution—Juvenile literature.
4. Gays—Nazi persecution—Juvenile literature. 5. Holocaust, Jewish (1939-
1945)—Juvenile literature.] I. Title. II. Series.
    D803.A495 2003
    940.53'18—dc21
                            2002151085

Printed in the United States of America

10 9 8 7 6 5 4 3 2

To Our Readers: We have done our best to make sure all Internet Addresses in this
book were active and appropriate when we went to press. However, the author and
the publisher have no control over and assume no liability for the material available on those Internet sites or on other Web sites they may link to. Any comments
or suggestions can be sent by e-mail to comments@enslow.com or to the address
on the back cover.

Illustration Credits: Andras Tsagatakis, courtesy of USHMM Photo Archives, p. 22;
Archives of Mechanical Documentation, Warsaw, Poland, courtesy of USHMM
Photo Archives, p. 3; Bezirkskrankenhaus Kaufbeuren, courtesy of USHMM Photo
Archives, p. 15; courtesy of USHMM Photo Archives, pp. 5, 11, 12, 19, 20, 24, 27,
34, 37, 41, 47, 58, 65, 72; Deutsches Historisches Museum, courtesy of USHMM
Photo Archives, p. 13; Eliezer and Jenelly Rosenberg, courtesy of USHMM Photo
Archives, p. 52; Enslow Publishers, Inc., p. 26; Harry Lore, courtesy of USHMM
Photo Archives, p. 38; Harry S. Truman Library, courtesy of USHMM Photo
Archives, p. 63; KZ Gedenkstaette Dachau, courtesy of USHMM Photo Archives,
pp. 75, 78, 82, 87; Library of Congress, pp. 6, 29, 42, 43, 48, 54, 55, 68; Library of
Congress, courtesy of USHMM Photo Archives, p. 50; Lorenz Schmuhl, courtesy of
USHMM Photo Archives, p. 1; Main Commission for the Prosecution of the Crimes
against the Polish Nation, courtesy of USHMM Photo Archives, pp. 31, 33, 70;
Muzej Revolucije Narodnosti Jugoslavije, courtesy of USHMM Photo Archives,
pp. 57, 64; Muzeum Sztuki w Lodzi, courtesy of USHMM Photo Archives, p. 69;
National Archives, pp. 2, 8, 77; National Archives, courtesy of USHMM Photo
Archives, 40 (both); National Museum of American Jewish History, courtesy of
USHMM Photo Archives, p. 9; Robert A. Schmuhl, courtesy of USHMM Photo
Archives, p. 17, 36; Zydowski Instytut Historyczny Instytut Naukowo-Badawczy,
courtesy of USHMM Photo Archives, p. 84.

Cover Illustration: Archives of Mechanical Documentation, Warsaw, Poland,
courtesy of USHMM Photo Archives

3/05   P+T   26.60

Contents

Introduction: World War II
and the Holocaust   7

1 Building the "Master Race" 11

2 The Polish Victims 27

3 The Russian Campaign 43

4 The Gypsies of Europe 57

5 The Race Criminals 75

Timeline 90

Chapter Notes 92

Glossary 97

Further Reading 100

Internet Addresses 101

Index 102

World War II began in 1939 when the German army attacked Poland under the direction of Adolf Hitler.

Introduction
World War II and
the Holocaust

On September 1, 1939, German troops invaded Poland. Two days later, Britain and France declared war on Germany. World War II had begun. Under Adolf Hitler and his National Socialist German Workers' Party, also called the Nazi party, Germany would soon conquer most of Europe.

Hitler planned to build a *Reich*, or empire, that would last for a thousand years. He believed that Northern Europeans, or Aryans as he called them, were a master race—a group of people superior to others.

Hitler falsely believed that some people were inferior, such as Jews, Gypsies, Poles, Russians, and people of color. These people would be given no rights in his Reich. Some would be exterminated, or killed. Others would be kept alive only so long as they served their Aryan masters. It was a dark and terrible vision that cost millions of lives.

In the early days of the war, Germany seemed unbeatable. One nation after another fell to the German *blitzkrieg*, or "lightning war." The Nazis conquered Poland in just twenty-six days. Denmark, Norway, Belgium, the Netherlands, and France fell in the spring of 1940.

By the end of 1940, the Germans had occupied most of Western Europe and made alliances with Italy and Japan. The Axis, as this alliance was called, soon conquered parts of Asia, Eastern Europe, and North Africa.

In 1941, the picture changed. In June, Germany invaded the Soviet Union, now called Russia. America entered the war on December 7, when Japan attacked the United States naval base in Pearl Harbor, Hawaii. The Germans soon found themselves fighting

Japan attacked the United States naval base in Pearl Harbor on December 7, 1941. Shown here is the explosion of the USS *Shaw*.

German trains carried victims to death camps. The killing continued even as Germany realized it was going to be defeated.

the British and the Americans in the West, and the Soviets in the East. They also devoted men and resources to exterminating Jews and other people the Nazis saw as inferior.

Even when the war turned against Germany, this slaughter did not stop. Trains that could have carried troops and supplies to the fighting fronts were used instead to transport victims to death camps. The killing continued until the last possible moment.

After Germany surrendered on May 7, 1945, survivors began telling what they had suffered. Pictures of starving prisoners, mass graves, and gas chambers disguised as showers appeared in newspapers and movie newsreels. People all over the world were horrified.

As survivors told their stories, the horror grew. New words came into the language. Old words took on new meanings. Holocaust came to represent mass murder on a scale that had never been seen before. Genocide described the systematic killing of specific racial or ethnic groups.

These words are reminders of a grim truth—human beings can do terrible things to one another. This is why knowing about the Holocaust is so important. Knowledge is the best defense against the hatred that produced the Nazi racial state and caused the death of innocent millions.

Building the "Master Race"

When Adolf Hitler became chancellor of Germany in 1933, his plans for the future went beyond building an empire. He wanted to create a Germanic master race. These Aryans, as Hitler called them, would be tall, blond warriors, born to conquer and to rule.

Hitler described this superior human being in remarks about his vision for German youth: "A violently active, dominating, [fearless], brutal youth—that is what I am after."[1]

The Nazis would go to any lengths to build this warlike master race. Their racial policy included eliminating or enslaving groups they considered inferior and purifying their own Aryan racial stock.

The German people themselves were the first victims of this plan. In the name of racial health, Germans with inherited defects were sterilized so they could not have children. Thousands of mentally retarded and mentally ill people were killed in the so-called euthanasia (mercy killing) program. Undesirables such as homosexuals, abortionists, and racially-intermarried Germans were imprisoned or even killed as race criminals.

This racial health program was followed by the mass murder that has come to be known as the Holocaust. Jews were the chief victims, but millions of others also suffered.

Thousands of mentally retarded and mentally ill people, such as these children, were killed in euthanasia centers.

Jews were the primary victims of the Nazis. This poster advertises an issue of an anti-Semitic newspaper published in Germany.

In the name of racial purity, the Nazis killed half the Gypsy population of Europe. They slaughtered millions of Poles, Russians, and other Slavic peoples.

Building the Nazi "Racial State"

Race is supposed to account for inborn physical differences that set human groups apart from one another. There have been many different systems of racial classification. Some identify three major races: African, European, and Asian. Others have created as many as two hundred distinctive racial groups. According to one anthropologist, "'Race' has many meanings for many people. Probably the only thing about race that is clear is that we are confused about the origins and proper use of the term."[2]

The Nazi system of racial classification put northern Europeans, or Aryans, as Hitler called them, at the top of the ladder. Other white-skinned peoples stood below, followed by people of color and then by Jews.

To the Nazis, race not only determined physical traits, but mental ability and character as well. Thus, Poles, Russians, and other Slavic peoples were considered dull-minded and suited only to hard labor. Gypsies were born thieves and liars. People of color, such as Africans and Asians, were scarcely human at all.

Racist ideas cropped up everywhere in German society. The average person could not get through a day without reading or hearing about race. It was on the radio and in the newspapers. Children learned about it in school.

Teachers and textbooks presented Nazi ideas about race and heredity as proven facts. Typical homework assignments from a racial hygiene textbook included the following: "Summarize the spiritual characteristics of

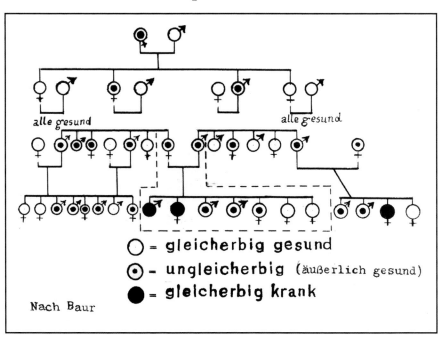

O = gleicherbig gesund

⊙ = ungleicherbig (äußerlich gesund)

● = gleicherbig krank

Nach Baur

Nazi ideas about race and heredity were taught as facts in schools. This family tree illustrates which members of a family carry the gene for a hereditary illness.

the individual races." " . . . Collect propaganda posters and caricatures [cartoons] for your race book and arrange them according to a racial scheme."[3]

The open racism of these assignments was also reflected in materials for adults. For example, one scholarly text noted that non-Nordic humans ranked halfway between the Nordic (northern European) peoples and "the great apes . . . We could also call non-Nordic Man a [primitive]; however, the term 'sub-human' is better."[4]

Controlling Heredity

Forced sterilization was the first of the Nazi racial programs. The exact mechanisms, or workings, of heredity were not well understood. However, scientists did know that genes could pass traits from one generation to the next.

Heredity explains why children resemble their parents and why elephants don't give birth to kangaroos. It also explains why certain diseases and disabilities run in families. One generation passes faulty genes to the next. When this happens, children may be born with crippling defects.

The idea of improving humankind by preventing people with "bad genes" from having children did not start with the

Nazis. Nineteenth-century British scientist Francis Galton reasoned that humankind could be improved if people with good heredity had more children than people with bad heredity.

In 1883, he coined the word "eugenics" (from the Greek: "good in birth") to describe this selective breeding. His work started a eugenics movement that enjoyed wide popularity in Britain and the United States during the early twentieth century.

In Germany, the Nazis found that eugenics fit right into their racial policies. Less than a year after Adolf Hitler came to power, the

The Nazis attempted to prevent people with genetic defects from having children. Disabled and ill prisoners were sterilized, sometimes without their knowledge.

Law for the Prevention of Genetically Diseased Offspring was enacted. It required sterilization for people with genetic defects.

Many people were sterilized without their consent and some without their knowledge. Because surgical sterilization was time-consuming and expensive, the Nazis tried mass methods. In one such experiment, subjects were seated at desks and told to fill out lengthy questionnaires. While they worked at this task, machines hidden beneath the seats focused Xrays on their genitals, producing sterility.

About four hundred thousand Germans were sterilized during the Nazi era. Those who knew, or found out, about the procedure were told to consider it a "sacrifice in the interests . . . of the Volk [German people]."[5]

"Life Unworthy of Life"

From preventing unwanted births, the Nazis moved to direct killing of "useless" people. The euthanasia, or mercy death, project began with severely handicapped newborns. The Nazi leaders had discussed the possibility of medical killing; Hitler himself was said to approve of the idea. However, nothing was done until one exceptional case came to the Führer's attention.

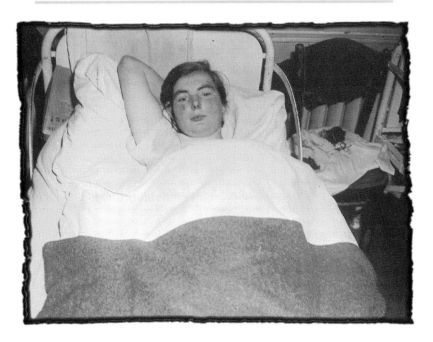

The Nazis not only prevented births through sterilization, but they killed people they considered useless. Elizabeth Killiam was sterilized by the Nazis before being brought to a euthanasia center to be killed.

In late 1938, a distraught father wrote to Hitler about his infant son, born blind and severely retarded, with one leg and part of an arm missing. The father asked permission to have the baby put to a merciful death.

Hitler decided that this man's plight would make a good test case. He sent his personal physician, Karl Brandt, to investigate. Brandt consulted with other doctors on the case. He saw the baby for himself. And he gave permission for the euthanasia to proceed. To the doctors who would do the actual killing,

Karl Brandt was Hitler's personal physician. He developed a euthanasia program with Hitler's approval and was actively involved in the project.

he gave Hitler's personal guarantee—they would not face prosecution.

The Führer was pleased with the outcome of this case. He authorized Brandt to develop a program for similar cases. The Nazi euthanasia project had begun.

On August 18, 1939, the government ordered hospital maternity wards to report handicapped newborns. The conditions listed included mental retardation, "deformations of any kind," and paralysis.[6] This order also required doctors to "register all children who suffer from any of the [listed] conditions . . . and who are not older than three years of age."[7]

These reports were supposed to be used for research. Actually, a committee went over them to decide who should live and who should die. Children selected for death could be taken from their homes. The parents were told that this was for expert treatment. To keep up this ruse, killing centers were set up in existing institutions, such as mental hospitals and homes for the handicapped.

> 'Treatment' included poison gas, overdoses of morphine, and occasionally the direct injection of phenol (a substance which stops the heart). Families received death certificates listing the cause of death as pneumonia, typhus . . . seizures, and other natural causes.[8]

Hartheim Institute was one of six hospitals and nursing facilities used by the Nazis for their euthanasia program.

A separate program targeted mentally ill, mentally retarded, and severely handicapped adults. Code-named T4 for its office address at Tiergartenstrasse 4 in Berlin, the program grew to include six major killing centers. They were equipped with gas chambers disguised as showers. Many of the personnel who would operate the death camps of the Final Solution received their training in the T4 killing centers.

When the T4 program officially ended in August 1941, it was under fire from outraged citizens. One psychiatrist explained, "Family members of patients wrote . . . expressing confusion and pain . . . [and] resentment about relatives not . . . having 'a chance to say goodbye.'"[9]

Some families filed formal charges. One judge who received some of these complaints wrote to the minister of justice. He said that "man commits an act of . . . extraordinary arrogance when he takes it upon himself to put an end to a human life because, with his limited understanding, he can no longer grasp the entire meaning of that life."[10]

In August 1941, Hitler issued a stop order, closing the T4 killing centers. By that time, more than seventy thousand adults and five hundred children had been killed.

Wild Euthanasia

The order that closed the T4 gas chambers did not stop the killing. It just closed the gas chambers and disbanded the central T4 project. The killing continued by other means.

It became known as wild euthanasia—killing that occurred without written orders or central planning. According to one historian, "after the stop order physicians and nurses killed . . . with [pills], injections, and starvation. In fact, more victims of euthanasia [died] after the stop order was issued than before.[11]

Wild euthanasia took place in hospitals throughout Germany. For some doctors and

G 1

30173

Sterbeurkunde.

(Standesamt der Freien Hansestadt Bremen   Nr, 3496/1938)

Sarah Selma Zwienicki, geb. Stiefel, mosaisch,
— — — — — ,

wohnhaft in Bremen, — — — — — ,

ist am 10.November 1938   um 4   Uhr — — — Minuten

in   Bremen tot aufgefunden worden.— — — — — — verstorben. —
— — — —

Die Verstorbene war geboren am 8. Juni 1882

in   Hamburg, — — — —

(Standesamt Hamburg   Nr. ?)

Vater: Koppel Stiefel, — — — — —

Mutter: Elise geb. Cohen — — — —

Die Verstorbene war —nicht— verheiratet mit dem Fahrradhändler
Josef Zwienicki. — — — —

Bremen , den 23. November 19 38.

Der Standesbeamte
In Vertretung.

[signature]

Deaths that were carried out under the euthanasia program were included in normal reports of fatalities. False causes of death were listed on death certificates and did not appear unusual.

nurses, killing handicapped patients became just another part of hospital routine. The deaths were included in normal reports of fatalities. With a false but believable cause of death, they did not appear unusual.

The euthanasia projects forged a link between killing and healing. Doctors even used the vocabulary of medicine to describe their killings. Victims were patients who received therapy or treatment. A deadly injection was a sedative to help the patient sleep, and purposeful starvation was a special diet. Surrounded by the language of healing, doctors grew accustomed to medicalized murder. For some, destroying a "useless" person for the good of the German *Volk* came to seem as normal as cutting out a diseased appendix to save a patient's life.

From killing thousands because they were disabled, the Nazis moved to killing millions because they were "subhuman." With the beginning of World War II, Nazi racism went beyond murderous doctors and nurses. In the name of Aryan superiority, it transformed the German nation into a killing machine.

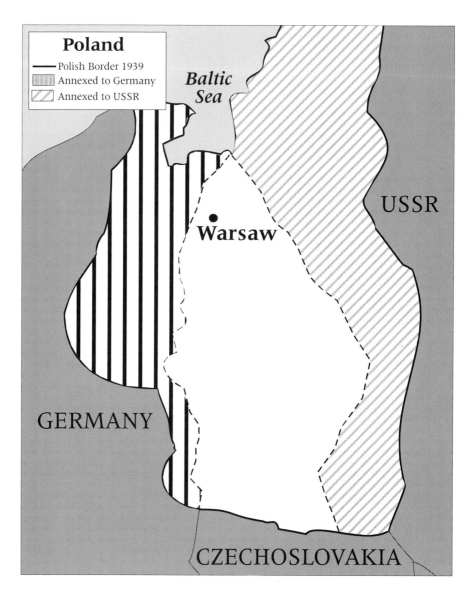

Poland

— Polish Border 1939

▦ Annexed to Germany

▧ Annexed to USSR

Baltic Sea

USSR

• Warsaw

GERMANY

CZECHOSLOVAKIA

In a secret agreement, Hitler and Stalin divided Poland between Germany and the Soviet Union (USSR). This map shows how the country was divided after Germany attacked Poland in 1939.

The Polish Victims

Before the German invasion of Poland on September 1, 1939, began World War II, Adolf Hitler told his generals what he planned to do. "I have sent to the east . . . my 'Death Head Units' [SS troops], with the order to kill without mercy all men, women, and children of Polish race or language. Only in such a way will we win the [living] space we need."[1]

This set the tone for Germany's war against Poland. It was not to be an ordinary war: a political and military struggle between enemy states. It did not end when Poland surrendered and German troops occupied Polish territory. Instead, it became a war against the Polish people and Polish culture, or in Nazi terms, a racial war.

The Poles are a Slavic people. The term Slav refers to culture and language, not race. Slavic peoples migrated out of Asia in the third or second century B.C., to settle in eastern and southeastern Europe. Their modern descendants include eastern Europeans such as Russians, Ukrainians, Belorussians, and Czechs, as well as Poles.

The Invasion of Poland

Before sending German troops into Poland, Hitler mapped out a careful plan. He began by seeking a non-aggression pact with Soviet dictator Josef Stalin.

This appeared to be a strange alliance. Hitler hated communists and Russians; Stalin was both. However, the Führer was not above dealing with anyone who could be useful to him. Before moving on Poland, he needed to be sure the Soviets would stay out of the fight.

On August 23, 1939, the Hitler-Stalin pact was signed. Both leaders promised not to go to war with one another, or to help one another's enemies. In a separate and secret agreement, they carved up Poland and most of Eastern Europe. Hitler pledged to stay out of eastern Poland. He also promised not to invade small nations such as Latvia and

In 1939, Hitler made a pact with Soviet dictator Josef Stalin, shown here. This enabled Hitler to move forward with his plans.

Lithuania, which shared a common border with the Soviet Union (USSR).

With the Soviets out of the way, Hitler felt free to move eastward, across the German-Polish border. Some of his advisors warned that there was still danger from the west.

Britain and France had treaties with Poland. If they honored those treaties, they would come to Poland's aid. Hitler brushed aside these concerns. Neither the British nor the French had lifted a finger when Germany annexed Austria and later took the Sudetenland from Czechoslovakia. Hitler did not think they would now risk all-out war to save Poland.

For extra insurance, Hitler planned to make the conflict look like Poland's fault. On the night of August 31, 1939, SS troops staged fake attacks along the German-Polish border. They dressed in Polish uniforms and used Polish weapons. They even arranged for casualties. Concentration camp prisoners dressed as Polish soldiers were killed and left lying on the ground. Their bodies "proved" that Poland had been the aggressor.

Hitler expressed outrage at this "unprovoked attack." The Poles had left him no choice but to fight, he claimed. In the predawn hours of September 1, German soldiers invaded Poland. They struck with overwhelming force: blitzkrieg, or "lightning war," Hitler called it.

Ground troops with tanks and heavy artillery swept through the countryside. Planes bombed and fired on cities, villages, and even shepherds in the fields. At one point, Polish cavalry, or horse-mounted troops, made a counterattack. It was brave and bold, but hopeless. Most of them died in withering fire.

The British and French did not behave as Hitler had expected. On September 3, both nations declared war on Germany. However,

German troops attacked Poland on September 1, 1939. These blindfolded Polish prisoners are being led to an execution site by SS guards.

neither of them sent troops to help the Poles. That was a mistake.

Between them, British and French troops outnumbered the Germans nearly three to one. As one historian pointed out, "The war could have taken a different course and Nazi atrocities [acts of murder, cruelty and violence] may never have taken place."[2] Had Britain and France attacked, they might have halted the invasion of Poland almost before it began.

As Germany battered Poland from the west, the Soviet Union invaded the eastern part of the country. By September 28, the Polish nation was completely occupied.

German-controlled Poland was further divided into two parts—a western region, which was annexed, or joined, directly to Germany, and an occupation zone known as General Government. In both areas, the Nazi assault on Polish nationhood and cultural identity soon began.

The Plan for Poland

The Nazis planned to kill, expel, or enslave Polish nationals so German settlers could take their lands and property. Germans needed *lebensraum*, or "living space," Hitler claimed. They would take part of it from the Poles.

The Nazis took many Polish prisoners and took their land and property. This Polish POW stands at attention during roll call at a concentration camp.

The Führer's orders to Hans Frank, Governor-general of the occupied zone, made this clear. He told Frank "to reduce it [Poland] to a heap of rubble in its economic, social, cultural and political structure."[3]

Brutal though this order was, it stopped short of total extermination. This was the chief difference in Nazi attitudes toward Jews and Poles. Jews were an infection that must be destroyed. Poles were an inferior group that could be exploited.

Hans Frank, right, was governor-general of the occupied Poland. Frank and Heinrich Himmler, left, were two of Hitler's top Nazi officials.

Though millions of Poles would be killed, some would be kept alive to serve as slaves. Polish slaves would be "reduced to an animal state" of living. "Hitler [planned to] educate the Poles only up to the fourth grade. Instructors would teach Poles to count up to 500, write their names, and be obedient to the Germans."[4]

The Fate of Educated Poles

After conquering Polish territory, the Nazis began the systematic destruction of Polish culture. They started with the most educated part of the population. These were the people who could not be easily controlled.

The SS began by arresting about two hundred professors and teachers at the Jagiellonian University in Kracow. These scholars were sent to concentration camps, where many of them died. Not long afterward, all Polish universities and high schools were closed. According to Hans Frank, governor-general of occupied Poland, schools were no longer necessary for Poles.

In the spring of 1940, Frank created a plan to coordinate exterminations throughout the General Government. By the end of May 1940, over two thousand people had been arrested and killed. Governor-general Frank wanted more. At a meeting on May 30, he called upon the security police to "take the most rigorous measures possible."[5]

These rigorous measures included actions against the Catholic Church. Because the Church played an important role in Polish national life, the Nazis regarded it as a threat. They killed some four thousand Polish priests and sent nearly four thousand more to concentration camps. They closed two thousand churches.

Doctors were also important targets. In the world of the Nazi Reich, or empire, there was no need to waste medical resources on sick Poles. The Nazis closed hundreds of hospitals and medical clinics. They arrested thousands

of doctors and medical students.

Dr. Stanley M. Garstka was studying at Warsaw University when he was arrested and taken to Pawiak prison. Years later, he remembered his arrest in painful detail:

The Nazis killed thousands of priests and closed churches. This clergyman stands at roll call in a concentration camp.

36

A priest and several nuns stand with a group of children at a convent in Poland, where the Jewish children were hidden during the German occupation.

I was ordered to undress, my head was shaved and I was [subjected to a] painfully forceful stream of cold water from the water hose . . . Alone and shivering from cold, behind an iron door in a small unheated cell . . . I was kept in isolation for three days.[6]

When Dr. Garstka was put into the general prison population, he met his favorite university professor. "Professor Kopec . . . told me that . . . we have to be prepared that the Germans will murder us in their action to destroy Poland's educated people."[7]

Many Poles were sent to concentration camps or forced to work hard labor. These Polish and Jewish prisoners are being forced to stand in a line with their arms raised.

Dr. Garstka survived Pawiak prison and eventually, the war. Professor Kopec did not. He was executed at Pawiak in March 1941.

Depopulating Poland

Killing thousands of educated Poles was only the beginning for the Nazis. They also wanted to reduce the overall Polish population. The new, "Germanized" Poland would have no place for "useless" Poles. Poles were expelled from their homes and lands, deported to concentration camps, and forced into hard labor on farms and in factories. They were starved, shot to death, and burned alive. Thousands of young adults were sterilized to reduce the number of Polish births.

In concentration camps and labor camps, Polish prisoners shared the fate of other inmates. They were controlled by terror and brutality and killed when they could no longer work. One Polish work detail at the Neuengamme concentration camp knew that every day one of them would be killed.

Some of the guards were always assigned to form a line around the work area to prevent escapes. Sooner or later, one of the Germans would grab a prisoner's cap off his head and throw it over the line. The victim was then forced to go after it. The moment he crossed

Prisoners were often required to perform hard labor. If they could no longer work, they were killed.

Guards enjoyed tormenting the prisoners. Many prisoners were killed trying to follow the guards orders.

the line, he would be shot dead. The guards thoroughly enjoyed this vicious game.

Over one million Poles died in concentration camps during the war. Two million were killed outside the camps. Poland itself was stripped of resources. In spite of all this, the Polish people and their culture survived. Their continued existence became one more defeat for the Nazi war machine, and for Adolf Hitler's racist dream of Aryan supremacy.

Vladimir Lenin of Russia, shown here, was said to have partly Jewish ancestry. Karl Marx also came from a Jewish background. As a result, Hitler thought of communism as a Jewish doctrine.

The Russian Campaign

Adolf Hitler never planned to keep the agreement he made with Soviet dictator Josef Stalin. The pact of August 1939 was a necessary evil, nothing more. It would keep the Soviets out of the way until Hitler himself could choose the time and place for a confrontation.

Hitler hated Russians and other Soviet peoples because they were Slavs and because they were Communists. In his mind, communism was a Jewish invention. Karl Marx, who developed the communist philosophy, came from a German-Jewish background. Vladimir Illyich Lenin, leader of the October 1917 revolution in Russia, was said to have partly Jewish ancestry. To Hitler, this was enough to make communism a Jewish doctrine and, therefore, a racial issue.

Nazis and Communists

On the surface, communism and Nazism seemed very different from one another. The Nazis wanted to build an empire ruled by an Aryan elite. The Communists wanted a dictatorship of the proletariat, or working class.

The two competing systems actually had a great deal in common. Both the Union of Soviet Socialist Republics (USSR) and Nazi Germany were totalitarian states. Both were ruled by dictators whose power was absolute. Both resorted to mass murder to gain their ends. Both emphasized the importance of struggle in human affairs.

Hitler regarded this struggle as biological; a life-or-death fight for what evolutionist Charles Darwin had called the survival of the fittest.

To Hitler, the principle was simple: the strong win, the weak lose. "It is not by the principles of humanity that man lives or is able to preserve himself above the animal world, but [only through] the most brutal struggle."[1] He would use this idea to justify everything from enslaving "subhuman" peoples to killing the handicapped.

The Communists took a more limited view of struggle. To them, the struggle that mattered in human affairs was between social classes. The ruling class used its wealth and power to exploit the working class. In the communist view, the Nazi idea of an Aryan master race was unthinkable. The struggle against Nazism was therefore necessary and justified.

Given the many conflicts between communism and Nazism, few people expected the Hitler-Stalin pact to last for long. The question was not *if* it would be broken, but when, and by which side.

Operation Barbarossa

As early as December 1940, Hitler was planning the invasion of Soviet Russia. It was code-named Operation Barbarossa, after the twelfth-century emperor Frederick I, called "Barbarossa," or "red beard."

Hitler planned in absolute secrecy. Outwardly, he was friendly toward Stalin. He played this role so well that the usually-wily Stalin ignored his own intelligence reports. A Czech agent sent word that German troops were massing in the East. Stalin called it a lie, meant to make trouble between him and Hitler. On the bottom of the report, he scrawled an order in angry red ink, "Find out where [this information] comes from and punish the culprit."[2]

Stalin was convinced that Germany would not attack Russia until it had finished with England. Hitler was too smart to open a second front in the East, Stalin claimed. So long as the war in the West continued, the Soviet Union would be safe.

While Stalin stubbornly ignored the threat from Germany, Hitler continued his plans. On March 30, 1941, he met with senior commanders and staff officers for Operation Barbarossa. Victory would be complete and total, he told them. German forces would wipe out the Soviet Army. There would also be a plan for dealing with Jews, Russian prisoners of war, and commissars, or Communist party officials.

In sealing the fate of millions of Russians, Hitler did not mince words:

> The war against Russia . . . is one of ideologies [beliefs] and racial differences and will have to be conducted with . . . unrelenting harshness. . . . The commissars are the bearers of ideologies directly opposed to National Socialism [Nazism]. Therefore the commissars will be liquidated [killed].[3]

As professional soldiers, the generals were supposed to follow a strict code of honor. Killing was to be confined to the battlefield. Honorable soldiers did not slaughter civilians or prisoners of war. Many of the generals later claimed they were horrified by the Führer's order. However, none of them uttered a word of protest against it.

The Nazi Invasion

German forces attacked the Soviet Union on June 22, 1941. They struck with such overwhelming force that victories were swift and easy. Stalin's refusal to believe that Hitler would invade had left the Russians unprepared.

Within hours of the opening attack, the *Luftwaffe*, or German Air Force, had destroyed

Germany attacked the Soviet Union in June of 1941. The Russians were unprepared for the attack.

more than one thousand Soviet planes. Most were bombed on the ground, never having made it into the air. The Luftwaffe also targeted centers of civilian population.

A survivor of an air raid on the city of Minsk explained what it was like:

> A squadron of ninety-six aircraft . . . bombed the town all day long. The entire [center of the city] was destroyed . . . During the bombardment we crept into the cellar. And then, when we came out, what did we see there! Burning houses, ashes, ruins. And corpses everywhere in the streets. People . . . could not flee [the city] quickly enough since the streets were jam packed. And those that were outside were mown down by low-flying German aircraft.[4]

The German aerial attack on the Soviet Union in 1941 involved planes such as this one.

Ground troops followed the aerial (air) bombardment. They came with heavy artillery and tens of thousands of men. With overwhelming force, they pushed the Soviet defenders steadily back.

Behind them came the *Einsatzgruppen* killing squads. These troops were charged with the dirty business of mass murder. They executed Jews and commissars immediately. They also killed thousands of people who were "useless" because of age, disability, or illness. Whole villages were destroyed, their populations killed or deported for slave labor.

The Nazis dehumanized the victim groups, or tried to make them seem less than human. They called Ukrainians and Russians "semi-savage inferiors, incapable of reason," who were more like "machines or animals than human beings."[5]

The Cost of Hatred

These "subhumans" turned out to be brave fighters. They retreated before the German onslaught, but they did not break and run. They regrouped after their first losses. Resistance stiffened.

Soon, German victories were neither so quick nor so easy. By the end of 1941, many Nazi leaders were beginning to realize that the Führer had been wrong; there would be

The Einsatzgruppen killing squads were responsible for mass murder. They killed thousands of people.

no swift victory in Russia. They faced a drawn-out war against an enemy that was fighting to protect its own soil.

They also faced a new enemy on the Western front. After Germany's Japanese allies attacked Pearl Harbor, Hawaii, on December 7, the United States came into the war.

Hitler's generals were worried about spreading their forces too thin. The Führer himself was not. He still believed that Aryan racial superiority would win the day. In the West, this belief led him to underestimate the importance of the United States' entry into the war. In the East, it led him to pass up chances to make alliances.

Many people in the Ukraine and the Baltic countries were not sympathetic to communism. They were not eager to be part of the Soviet Union. Some might have welcomed the Germans as liberators if local populations had not been so badly mistreated. Hitler could not see past his own racist hatred. To him, eastern Europeans were subhuman Slavs, fit only to be slaves for the German masters.

The POW Problem

This contempt for Slavs shaped the fate of Russian soldiers who fell into Nazi hands. The Germans killed "2.8 million young, healthy Soviet POWs in less than eight months."[6]

Some of these victims were force-marched hundreds of miles without shelter, warm clothing, or enough food. Those who fell by the wayside were shot where they lay. The survivors were taken to POW camps. Some of these "camps" were nothing but fenced enclosures without roofs, furniture, baths, or toilet facilities: "The prisoners had to lie in the sun, then in mud, and in the fall—with temperatures as low as minus 30 degrees centigrade (2 degrees fahrenheit)—faced the possibility of freezing to death."[7]

Millions of Soviet POWs were killed in a very short period of time. These Soviet POWs were captured near Wisznice, Poland.

Because of the terrible conditions in the camps, epidemics were common. An outbreak often became an excuse for wholesale murder. For example, in January 1942, an epidemic of spotted fever struck a POW camp in Estonia. Over fourteen hundred Russian inmates fell ill.

Medical officer Hans Deuschl wrote to SS chief Heinrich Himmler about the problem. He pointed out that only about 25 percent of the prisoners were physically able to work. There was also a danger that the disease would spread to German soldiers working in or near the camp.

Deuschl asked permission to take radical measures. He wanted to shoot half the Russian prisoners so the other half could receive more food and better care. In explaining this idea to Himmler, he did not mince words. "I would rather see the death of 500 [Communist] beasts (who will probably eventually die anyway—of hunger, cold, or disease), than see one German soldier . . . perish from epidemic disease."[8] Himmler granted the request.

The Turning Point

While Russian prisoners were dying by the thousands, their German enemies also faced a crisis. By the winter of 1941, Nazi troops

SS chief Heinrich Himmler (right), shown here with Hermann Göring, gave permission for the murder of thousands of Russian prisoners.

had fought their way to the outskirts of Moscow. Hitler expected the Russian capital to fall any day. The Soviets had other ideas. On December 6, they struck back, driving the Germans from Moscow.

Hitler blamed this defeat on the German military. The generals talked about caution, withdrawal, and retreat. They said it was impossible to fight a war in the depths of a Russian winter. Hitler would not listen.

On December 19, 1941, he personally took command of all German armed forces. He ordered field commanders in Russia "to stand

and fight where they were . . . [and refused] all requests to withdraw. . . . Officers who failed to obey [this order] were dismissed or court-martialled." [9]

While the army held, Hitler planned new offensives. He convinced himself that the Russians were weakening; that it was only a matter of time before their vast empire belonged to Germany.

No sacrifice was too great to achieve that goal. Hitler cared nothing for the thousands who would die. Victory was all that mattered.

German troops were defeated at Stalingrad on February 2, 1943. This was the beginning of defeat for Germany.

For Germany, the Führer's misjudgments would contribute to a crushing defeat. It came on February 2, 1943, when a ragtag band of German survivors surrendered to the Soviet Army at Stalingrad.

The defeat put an end to Germany's chances for victory in the East, but it did not put an end to the fighting or the dying. That would continue for more than two years.

By the time the war ended, 20 million Soviet citizens had lost their lives. The majority of that 20 million were not soldiers who died in battle. They were civilians— men, women, and children who died because the Nazis considered them unfit to live.

The Gypsies of Europe

For centuries, the people known as Gypsies roamed Europe. They had no home and wanted none. They preferred *lungo drom*, "the long road," where life was an endless journey to nowhere in particular.

Lungo drom meant freedom, but that freedom came at a price. Everywhere they roamed, the Gypsies were strangers. Settled folk regarded them with suspicion and sometimes with hatred. The Gypsies returned the favor; many of them did not think highly of the *gadje*, the outsiders, with their regular jobs and settled lives.

When the Nazis came to power, the Gypsies faced a new and deadly enemy. Nothing in their wanderings had prepared them for the racism of the Nazi killing machine.

Gypsies were another target of the Nazis. This Gypsy couple is in the Belzec concentration camp.

The Gypsy Mysteries

Gypsy is a European name for a group of loosely-related tribes. Most of the Gypsies in Germany and German-occupied Europe belonged to the Roma and Sinti tribes. These tribes were called Gypsies by Europeans who believed that they came out of Egypt.

Today, scholars believe that the ancestors of modern Gypsies came from northern India. In part, this is because of similarities in language. The Roma and Sinti languages have much in common with Sanskrit, the language of ancient India.

Just how or why the Gypsies left India and made their way to Eastern Europe is unknown. The Gypsies are an unlettered people, with no written or oral records of their past.

Throughout their long history, traditional Roma and Sinti have had little interest in learning to read and write. At best, literacy seemed unnecessary; at worst, it could be dangerous.

Education was for the gadje, not for Gypsies. Schools not only taught reading and writing, they taught a way of life the Gypsies did not want. Educated Gypsies were apt to trade their own traditions for the settled life of the gadje, giving up freedom for an ordered existence and lungo drom for a permanent address. Many of them married gadje, and raised their children with no regard for Gypsy ways.

Gypsy ways had no place at all in Nazi Germany. As a people, Gypsies were dark-skinned and therefore considered inferior. Culturally, they were misfits. They had no interest in politics, power, or gadje wars. They could not—or would not—follow orders, or march in lockstep with Hitler's new Germany. They simply did not belong, and for that they would pay a terrible price.

Evaluating the Gypsies

Dealing with Gypsies under the Reich race laws was not a simple matter. Who was, and who was not, a Gypsy? Lifestyle alone could not answer that question. Some Gypsies had settled down and taken more-or-less regular jobs. Some had intermarried with local populations. On the other hand, some non-Gypsies had taken up the wandering life.

To settle the question of Gypsy racial identity, the Nazis formed a research institute. Dr. Robert Ritter was chosen to head it. Before joining the Gypsy project, Ritter had done research on criminal biology. He had attempted to prove that criminal behavior was inherited; that certain individuals were born to be dishonest or violent.

He approached the study of Gypsies with this idea in mind. He began by putting together family histories on approximately twenty thousand individuals. From this data, he concluded that the Gypsies were a "primitive people," distinct from and inferior to "white" Europeans.[1]

According to Ritter, Gypsy wanderlust was "in the blood" and therefore unchangeable.[2] This was why efforts to settle large numbers of Gypsies had always failed. Those Gypsies who did settle down, Ritter said, presented a whole new set of problems. Many lived in slum districts where they intermarried with lower class non-Gypsies. The result was a criminal underclass of *Mischlinge*, or people of mixed ancestry.

Ritter considered the Mischlinge even worse than "pure blooded" Gypsies. He called them "a population of parasites who lacked ambition and were work-shy."[3] He claimed that most of them refused to have steady jobs. Even when forced to work, they were lazy and unreliable. Instead of working, they lived by begging, stealing, and scavenging; taking what they could find wherever they could find it. Thus, the Nazis lumped Gypsies together with career criminals and other social misfits. They were labeled antisocial, or *asozial* in German.

Combating the "Gypsy Nuisance"

Along with other asocials, Gypsies were frequent targets of crime prevention laws. On December 14, 1937, Minister of the Interior Wilhelm Frick announced a new crime prevention decree. It allowed the police to take asocials into protective custody, even if they had committed no crime.

Additional regulations explained the meaning of this decree: asocials were people who "demonstrate by their conduct, even if it is not criminal, that they are unwilling to adapt to the life of the community." This included people with no fixed address and those "without a criminal record who sought to escape the duty to work and became dependent for their support on the public."[4] Many Gypsies, who held no regular jobs, ended up in concentration camps because of this decree.

On January 26, 1938, Heinrich Himmler and the SS became involved in dealings with Gypsies and other asocials. As Germany was rearming for war, the need for workers became critical. Himmler ordered the Gestapo to begin arresting the "work-shy."

Because Gypsies as a group had been defined as asocial, they were automatically considered work-shy. Hundreds were arrested

Wilhem Frick, shown here, announced a decree that allowed the police to take Gypsies and other asocials into custody even if they had committed no crime.

and put into concentration camps, where they were forced to work for the Reich.

Officially, the operation against the work-shy was not based upon race. Many non-Gypsies ended up in concentration camps because they could not, or would not, hold steady jobs. However, these people were judged as individuals. Gypsies were judged as members of an inferior racial group.

If there was any doubt about the racial nature of Gypsy policies, Himmler erased it on December 8, 1938. In a circular titled

Hundreds of Gypsies were put into concentration camps and forced to work. These Serbs and Gypsies are being deported to the camps.

"Combating the Gypsy Nuisance," he said that "the proper method of attacking the Gypsy problem seems to be to treat it as a matter of race."[5]

Himmler therefore ordered that "all settled and non-settled Gypsies and also all vagrants living a Gypsy-like existence" be registered with the government.[6] Local police were to report all people who appeared to be "Gypsies or part-Gypsies" because of "their looks and appearance, customs or habits."[7]

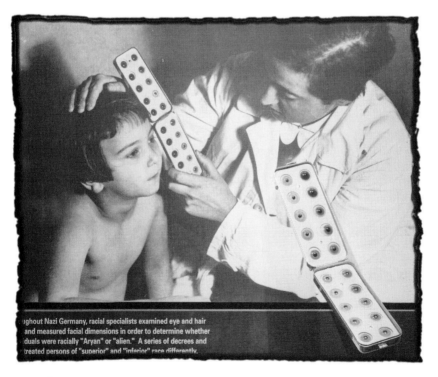

...ghout Nazi Germany, racial specialists examined eye and hair and measured facial dimensions in order to determine whether ...duals were racially "Aryan" or "alien." A series of decrees and ...treated persons of "superior" and "inferior" race differently.

Gypsies were forced to be registered with the government. They, and others, were subjected to exams to determine racial ancestry. This child is being given an eye color exam.

For reasons known only to him, Himmler was fascinated by the so-called racial characteristics of "Gypsy blood." At one point, he took an unusual interest in the Sinti tribe. He believed they were "purer blooded" than the Roma, because they had intermarried less with non-Gypsies. He toyed with the idea of setting up a "reservation" where these Gypsies would be kept as "living museum pieces."[8]

Later, he authorized an experiment with Gypsies in the Sachsenhausen concentration camp. He gave permission for Professor Werner Fischer to take blood samples from forty Gypsy subjects. The blood would be analyzed to see how it differed from the blood of other "races." These experiments were expected to produce "new insights into the nature of racial differences."[9]

Neither the blood studies nor the Sinti reservation scheme came to anything. If the studies were in fact performed, no report of them survived the war. As for preserving a "sample" of the Sinti, the people who deported Gypsies to concentration camps had neither the time nor the interest to worry about who was a Sinti and who a Roma. To them, a Gypsy was a Gypsy—and Gypsies did not belong in the Nazi racial state.

"The Devouring"

After German Gypsies were identified and registered, they were deported by the thousands to ghettos, concentration camps, and work camps. This was the beginning of *Porraimos*, "the devouring," which is the Gypsy name for the Holocaust.

Gypsies were usually separated from other prisoners. For example, in the Lodz ghetto, a special area was sealed off for them. The Nazis surrounded it with a double barbed wire fence and a ditch filled with water. A series of security posts dotted this formidable barrier.

Beginning on November 5, 1941, transports of Gypsies began arriving at the ghetto. Adolf Eichmann, the SS officer who arranged transports and train schedules, worked out a precise, five-day schedule. Every morning for four days, exactly one thousand Gypsy men, women, and children were packed into freight cars and sent to Lodz. On the fifth day, the count was one hundred and seven.

After allowing for the eleven people who died en route, the population of the Gypsy ghetto at Lodz went from zero to 4,096 in a five-day period. Many of these people soon died from starvation, disease, or other causes. According to one non-Gypsy witness, the

Adolf Eichmann was the SS officer who arranged the schedule for Gypsies being transported to the Lodz ghetto.

Nazis forced many Gypsies to hang members of their own families.

Those who did not die in the ghetto were among the first to be gassed at the Chelmno extermination camp. Altogether, the Lodz Gypsy ghetto lasted scarcely two months. None of the nearly five thousand residents survived.

Death was even swifter for the Gypsies of Russia. SS killing squads, called Einsatzgruppen, followed the regular army into the Soviet Union. The army's job was warfare; the Einsatzgruppen's job was mass

This is the Gypsy camp in the Lodz ghetto. All of the nearly five thousand people who were imprisoned here were killed.

murder. They slaughtered Gypsies along with Jews and Communists.

In some areas, Gypsies were easy to identify and separate from the rest of the population. Many Gypsy groups already camped off to themselves. Others gathered in the same neighborhoods. In these situations, the Einsatzgruppen wiped out whole communities, often in a single day.

Gypsies in Auschwitz/Birkenau

On December 16, 1942, Heinrich Himmler ordered mass deportation of Gypsies to the

This is a view of the kitchen barracks, the electrified fence, and the gate at the main camp of Auschwitz. Auschwitz II, where the Gypsies were sent, had a similar set up, but it was an extermination camp.

Auschwitz/Birkenau camp. This was nothing less than a death sentence. Birkenau, also known as Auschwitz II, was an extermination camp. Many who were sent there went straight to the gas chambers. Those who were not immediately killed were separated by sex and used for slave labor.

Gypsies went to a separate camp, where families were kept together. The exact reason for not breaking up Gypsy families is unknown. However, the presence of several generations together made the inmates ideal subjects for experiments and studies of various kinds.

Because of those "scientific" studies, one name has been forever linked with the Gypsies of Auschwitz/Birkenau. That name is Josef Mengele. He came to the camp as a young doctor with a desire to prove Nazi racial theories. He never achieved that goal. Instead, he created a legend of evil.

Mengele has been called a monster, a demon, an angel of death. This reputation grew out of the difference between what Mengele was and what he seemed to be. According to survivors, Mengele gave "the impression of [being] a gentle and cultured man who had nothing whatever to do with [the killing]." One person described him as "brutal, but in a gentlemanly, depraved

Josef Mengele was a feared Nazi doctor who performed experiments on camp prisoners.

[corrupt; wicked] way." Another noted that, "He could be friendly but kill." [10]

Mengele was fascinated by Gypsy children, especially twins. He treated them with kindness and even with affection. He gave them toys and treats, played games with them, and set up a kindergarten for the youngest ones. They called him "Uncle Pepi" and eagerly awaited his visits.

None of this stopped Mengele from personally killing fourteen pairs of Gypsy twins in a single night. One by one, he took them into his examining room and injected deadly phenol into their hearts. He then performed detailed autopsies, or after-death examinations, on the bodies.

By August 1944, the Allies were closing in on Germany. The British and Americans came from the west, the Soviets from the east. As conditions worsened for the SS, they decided to close down the Gypsy camp and exterminate its inhabitants. Mengele protested this decision. Up to the last, he tried to save at least his children. When he saw that this was impossible, he stopped protesting. Without a sign of guilt or grief, he loaded his own car with Gypsy children and drove them to the gas chambers.

Over half a million Gypsies died in the Porraimos, the great devouring. That is nearly one-third of the Gypsy population of Europe.

Most Gypsies are reluctant to talk about the Nazi era. Few of them openly wonder how a civilized nation could produce a place like Auschwitz, a man like Josef Mengele.

The people of lungo drom, the long road, are not given to worrying about the problem of evil. To them, evil is simply a part of life. Why an Auschwitz or a Mengele? Fifty years after the war, an unnamed Roma man gave a typically Gypsy answer to that question: "Every person is part Judas, part Christ. Only luck decides him."[11]

5

The Race Criminals

Not all victims of Nazi racism suffered because of their own racial identities. Many Germans ran afoul of the Nazis because they were less than enthusiastic in doing their racial duty to the Reich. People of good blood were expected to keep themselves in top physical shape and produce large families of blond, blue-eyed Aryan children.

Another group of Germans were punished because of whom they chose to love. Germans in homosexual or interracial relationships were guilty of "racial treason."[1] They could be imprisoned or even executed as race criminals.

Adolf Hitler and Homosexuals

In the early days of the Nazi party, homosexuals were tolerated. It was common knowledge within the Nazi party that SA commander Ernst Röhm and many of his top lieutenants were practicing homosexuals. Hitler himself defended them. When others within the party called for an investigation of Röhm's homosexual exploits, Hitler flatly refused.

The SA, he said, "is not an institute for the moral education of . . . young ladies, but a formation of seasoned fighters . . . [An SA man's] private life cannot be [investigated] unless it conflicts with basic principles of [Nazi] ideology."[2]

Hitler's loyalty to his SA commander only lasted as long as he needed the Stormtroops. When he won appointment as chancellor in 1933, Röhm became expendable. The crude and violent street fighter was fine in the beer halls of Munich. In the government halls of Berlin, he became an embarrassment.

In June 1934, Hitler ordered a purge. Over a three-day period, Ernst Röhm and nearly one hundred others were executed. To justify the blood-letting, Hitler claimed he was cleansing the SA of evil homosexual influences. He then banned homosexuality in all Nazi organizations. "I should like every mother to be able to allow her son to join the SA, [Nazi] Party, and Hitler Youth without fear that he may become morally corrupted in their ranks." To achieve this, Hitler ordered

Ernst Röhm, an SA commander, was a practicing homosexual. Early on, the Nazi party tolerated homosexuals.

all SA commanders and party leaders to expel homosexuals from their ranks. "I want to see men as SA commanders, not ludicrous monkeys."[3]

In keeping with the Führer's new orders, the *Gestapo*, the secret police unit of the SS, collected names of homosexuals all over Germany. In October 1934, they began making arrests. The Nazi war on homosexuals had begun.

Homosexuals all over Germany were arrested and sent to concentration camps.

The Homosexual Laws

The early arrests were made under an existing law against criminally indecent contact between males. This law, known as Paragraph 175, had been on the books since 1871. In 1935, the Nazis amended it with new and harsher regulations.

A later court decision gave judges broad powers to punish any behavior they considered offensive to the "inborn healthy instincts of the German people."[4] These offenses did not have to violate written law.

This put homosexuals at the mercy of the legal system. Even the most innocent acts could be defined as criminal and severely punished. As one young homosexual put it in a letter to a friend, "They can get you if you smile at another boy."[5]

SS Reichführer Heinrich Himmler became the chief Nazi crusader against homosexuals and other race criminals. Even by Nazi standards, Himmler had extreme views about race. In civilian life, he had studied agriculture and worked on a chicken farm. As a Nazi, he treated human reproduction almost as a problem in livestock breeding.

He despised homosexuals because they would not marry and have children. Also, he believed that they would recruit other men to their lifestyle. This would further reduce the number of males available for breeding. To Himmler, every German homosexual represented German children who would never be born. This made homosexuality into a racial hygiene issue. In a speech to SS trainees, Himmler made the following statement:

> There are those homosexuals who take the view: what I do is my business, a purely private matter. However, [these] things . . . are not the private affair of the individual, but signify the life and death of the nation, signify world power . . . [6]

In 1936, Himmler created the Reich Central Office for the Combating of Homosexuality and Abortion. Its offices were located in the Berlin headquarters of the Gestapo, the SS secret police unit. The new agency immediately began tracking and arresting homosexuals.

In this work, they faced a problem. Homosexuals were not as easy to identify as other victim groups. They could belong to any race or ethnic group, pursue any profession or job. In addition, they had long practice in hiding from a society that criminalized and rejected them.

The Gestapo dealt with this problem in its usual manner. Often, the arrest of a known homosexual led to the identification of others. The Gestapo scoured address books, letters, and mementoes for names. They also used a network of informers and encouraged private citizens to denounce suspected homosexuals. School children reported teachers; adults reported coworkers, neighbors, and even casual acquaintances.

These methods worked with deadly efficiency. Before the office was formed, homosexual arrests numbered in the hundreds; afterward, they numbered in the thousands. For example, the homosexual roundups of 1934 resulted in 766 convictions under Paragraph 175. In 1936, there were four thousand convictions and in 1938, eight thousand.[7]

Homosexuals in the Camps

At first, most men convicted of crimes under Paragraph 175 were sent to regular prisons. Beginning in 1937, those who completed their prison terms were not released. By order of Heinrich Himmler, they were transferred to concentration camps.

Marked by the pink triangle badges they were forced to wear in the camps, homosexuals became targets of exceptional brutality. A favorite method of killing them was to beat them to death. Homophobic, or homosexual-hating, guards and fellow prisoners would attack on the slightest excuse. Other prisoners could do nothing but stand and watch.

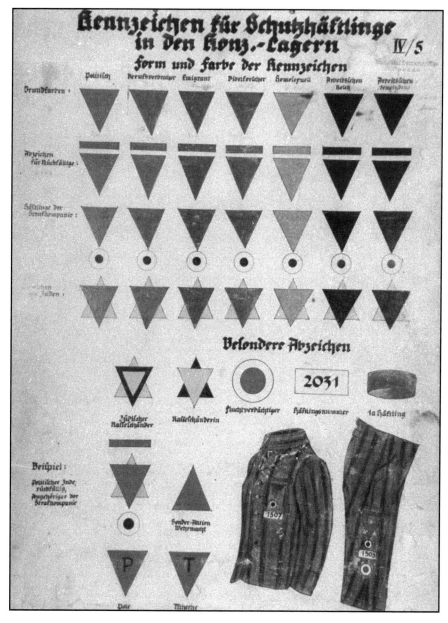

This is a chart of the different badges that prisoners were forced to wear in the camps. Homosexuals were made to wear pink triangle badges.

Because of such actions, death rates were high for homosexuals. About ten to fifteen thousand homosexual men were imprisoned in various camps throughout the Reich. Only about four thousand of them survived the war.[8]

At Sachsenhausen, the guards delighted in forcing homosexuals to do entirely meaningless work. According to survivor Heinz Heger,

> In the morning we had to cart the snow outside our block [barracks] from the left side of the road to the right side. In the afternoon we had to cart the same snow back from the right side to the left . . . We had to shovel up the snow with our [bare] hands . . . And so [it went], right thought the evening, and all at the double![9]

Ongoing Persecution

Even liberation and the end of the war did not necessarily mean freedom for homosexuals. Those who survived faced a whole new set of challenges. They were still viewed as criminals and social outcasts. Most laws and policies of the Nazi era were promptly repealed. Paragraph 175 was not. After Germany was divided into Eastern and Western sectors by the Allies, both governments continued to enforce it.

Homosexuals were no longer considered race traitors, but they were still considered

Homosexuals were often beaten and tortured in the camps. Thousands of homosexual men were murdered.

criminals. Those who had been convicted of offenses under Paragraph 175 still had to serve their sentences. Time in a concentration camp did not count as legal imprisonment.

The rest were set free, but many of them had nowhere to go. As one historian pointed out, they

> often did not return to a loving family or a group of sympathetic [friends] during the first months of readjustment. Families frequently refused to take [them] back . . . And former [homosexual] friends were usually displaced or dead . . . And like so many victims of the Third Reich, most [homosexuals] never recovered emotionally . . .[10]

Regulating Marriage and Family Life

Other than homosexuality, the most common forms of race treason were abortion and interracial marriage. Both were criminalized by Nazi race laws.

Abortion was already illegal when the Nazis came to power. It was allowed only if continuing the pregnancy would endanger the mother's life. The Nazi version of the law added another category; abortion was permissible for reasons of racial hygiene. If either parent had a hereditary defect, the pregnancy could be terminated.

Further changes in the existing law were made to stiffen penalties for illegal abortion. By 1937, doctors convicted of performing illegal abortions were commonly sentenced to ten years in prison and an additional ten years' loss of civil rights. Thus, for a period of twenty years, an abortion doctor would lose all the rights of German citizenship.

By 1939, unauthorized abortion was considered "a treason against the 'bodily fruit' of the German [race] . . . punishable in some cases by death."[11] These harsh laws applied only to Germans. Non-Aryans were allowed and even encouraged to get abortions.

Nazi race laws did not stop with abortion and homosexuality. In the autumn of 1935, the Nazis issued the Nuremberg Laws, named after the city where they were created. Two of these laws turned thousands of Germans into potential race traitors.

The Law for the Protection of German Blood and Honor banned marriage or sexual contact between Germans and Jews. It was later expanded to include relationships with other non-Aryan races.

Like many other Reich laws, this one was applied unevenly. Women were rarely charged with race crimes. The authorities assumed that men started and controlled these forbidden relationships.

Jews and other minorities were punished more severely than Aryans. Penalties for all classes of offenders became harsher over time. In the early days of the law, men

Jews and other minorities were punished severely. This
prisoner is forced to stand for hours without moving.

convicted of race pollution were imprisoned. After the beginning of the war in 1939, many were executed, often for trivial crimes. In one 1942 case, for example, the court sentenced a Jewish man to death because he "had kissed and embraced a woman 'of German blood.'" [12]

Not only interracial relationships were outlawed under the Nuremberg Laws. The Marital Health Law set limits on marriage for all Germans. People with sexually transmitted diseases could not marry. Neither could those with defects the Nazis considered hereditary.

Applicants for a marriage license had to pass genetic health exams. In cases where both partners had hereditary defects, they could sometimes get permission to marry by agreeing to be sterilized. There was also a provision for appeal. People who failed the exam could ask a genetic health court to review the case.

Beyond this, there was no further recourse, or source of help. Those who defied the law to marry in secret were subject to imprisonment for racial pollution. The marriage would be annulled, or declared invalid.

The Nazi Legacy

Many of the Nazi race laws and practices were not original. Other nations have also considered their enemies less than human.

Other nations have outlawed interracial relationships, homosexuality, and abortion. They have set standards for people wishing to marry.

However, the Nazis stand alone in making these racial policies the foundation of their whole society. Race, as they defined it, became the basis for judging the worth of all human beings. Fortunately for the world, they failed to build an Aryan empire or prove their own superiority. All they managed to do was demonstrate how an entire society can be corrupted by false ideas.

Timeline

January 30, 1933—Adolf Hitler appointed chancellor of Germany.

July 14, 1933—Law for the Prevention of Genetically Diseased Offspring (sterilization law) enacted.

October, 1934—Gestapo roundup of homosexuals begins.

September 15, 1935—Nuremberg Laws are announced.

July 12, 1936—First arrests of German Gypsies.

October 26, 1936—Reich Central Office for the Combating of Homosexuality and Abortion is established in Berlin.

December 14, 1937—Preventive crime fighting decree allows widespread arrests of Gypsies and other "asocials."

December 1938—All Gypsies required to register with police.

December 8, 1938—Heinrich Himmler issues circular on "Combating the Gypsy Nuisance."

September 1939—Germany invades Poland. Killings and deportations of Polish citizens begins.

October 1939—Hitler authorizes T4 euthanasia program.

June 22, 1941—Germany invades Soviet Union.

June 23, 1941—Mass executions of Jews, Gypsies, and Communist officials begin.

August 1941—Hitler issues stop order for T4 euthanasia centers.

December 7, 1941—Japanese attack on Pearl Harbor. United States enters war.

December 19, 1941—Hitler assumes personal command of all German armed forces.

June 6, 1944—"D-Day"; Allies invade continental Europe at Normandy, France.

May 7, 1945—Germany surrenders; war in Europe ends.

Chapter Notes

Chapter 1. Building the "Master Race"

1. Quoted in Hermann Rauschning, *The Voice of Destruction* (New York: G.P. Putnam's Sons, 1940), pp. 251–252.

2. Quoted in Eugenia Shanklin, *Anthropology & Race* (Belmont, Calif.: Wadsworth Publishing Co., 1994), p. 16.

3. Quoted in George L. Mosse, *Nazi Culture: Intellectual, Cultural and Social Life in the Third Reich* (New York: Schocken Books, 1981), p. 79.

4. Quoted in James M. Glass, *"Life Unworthy of Life": Racial Phobia and Mass Murder in Hitler's Germany* (New York: Basic Books, 1997), p. 55.

5. Robert N. Proctor, *Racial Hygiene: Medicine Under the Nazis* (Boston: Harvard University Press, 1988), p. 102.

6. United States Holocaust Memorial Museum, *In Pursuit of Justice: Examining the Evidence of the Holocaust* (Washington, D.C.: United States Holocaust Memorial Council, n.d.), p. 78.

7. Ibid.

8. Glass, p. 61.

9. Robert Jay Lifton, *The Nazi Doctors: Medical Killing and the Psychology of Genocide* (New York: Basic Books, Inc., 1986), p. 89.

10. Ibid., p. 89.

11. Henry Friedlander, *The Origins of Nazi Genocide: From Euthanasia to the Final Solution* (Chapel Hill, N.C.: University of North Carolina Press, 1995), p. 151.

Chapter 2. The Polish Victims

1. Quoted in Margot Stern Strom and William S. Parsons, *Holocaust and Human Behavior* (Watertown, Mass.: International Educations, 1982), p. 319.

2. M.I. Zawadzki, Ph.D., "The Genocide of the Poles," (Torrance, Calif.: Polish American Cultural Network, 1987), p. 3.

3. Joachim E. Fest, *The Face of the Third Reich: Portraits of the Nazi Leadership* (New York: Da Capo Press, 1999), p. 216.

4. *Model Curriculum for Human Rights and Genocide* (Sacramento, Calif.: California State Board of Education, 1987), p. 54.

5. Quoted in William L. Shirer, *The Rise and Fall of the Third Reich* (New York: Simon and Schuster, 1959), p. 876.

6. Stanley M. Garstka, "Polish Victims of the Holocaust: Personal Reflections Forty Years Later," transcription of an address, (Torrance, Calif.: Polish American Cultural Network, n.d.), p. 4.

7. Ibid.

Chapter 3. The Russian Campaign

1. Quoted in Joachim E. Fest, *The Face of the Third Reich: Portraits of the Nazi Leadership* (New York: Da Capo Press, 1999), p. 10.

2. Quoted in John Toland, *Adolf Hitler* (New York: Anchor Books, 1992), p. 657.

3. Quoted in William L. Shirer, *The Rise and Fall of the Third Reich* (New York: Simon and Schuster, 1959), pp. 1088–1089.

4. Quoted in Michael Burleigh, *The Third Reich: A New History* (New York: Hill and Wang, 2000), p. 488.

5. Bohdan Wytwycky, *The Other Holocaust: Many Circles of Hell* (Washington, D.C.: Novak Report on the New Ethnicity, 1980), p. 55.

6. Daniel Jonah Goldhagen, *Hitler's Willing Executioners: Ordinary Germans and the Holocaust* (New York: Alfred A. Knopf, 1996), p. 290.

7. Hamburg Institute for Social Research, *The German Army and Genocide: Crimes Against War Prisoners, Jews, and Other Civilians, 1939–1944* (New York: The New Press, 1999), p. 142.

8. Quoted in Robert N. Proctor, *Racial Hygiene: Medicine Under the Nazis* (Boston: Harvard University Press, 1988), p. 219.

9. Alan Bullock, *Hitler: A Study in Tyranny* (New York: Bantam, 1961), p. 597.

Chapter 4. The Gypsies of Europe

1. Guenter Lewy, *The Nazi Persecution of the Gypsies* (New York: Oxford University Press, 2000), p. 47.

2. Ibid.

3. Ibid.

4. Ibid., pp. 25–26.

5. Quoted in Michael Burleigh and Wolfgang Wipperman, *The Racial State: Germany 1933–1945* (New York: Cambridge University Press, 1992), p. 120.

6. Ibid.

7. Ibid.

8. Henry Friedlander, *The Origins of Nazi Genocide: From Euthanasia to the Final Solution* (Chapel Hill, N.C.: University of North Carolina Press, 1995), p. 293.

9. Quoted in Lewy, p. 179.

10. Quoted in Robert Jay Lifton, *The Nazi Doctors: Medical Killing and the Psychology of Genocide* (New York: Basic Books, Inc., 1986), pp. 343, 355.

11. Quoted in Isabel Fonseca, *Bury Me Standing: The Gypsies and Their Journey* (New York: Random House, Inc., 1996), p. 241.

Chapter 5. The Race Criminals

1. Richard Plant, *The Pink Triangle: The Nazi War against Homosexuals* (New York: Henry Holt and Co., 1986), p. 212.

2. Ibid., p. 60.

3. Quoted in Hans Peter Bleuel, *Sex and Society in Nazi Germany* (Philadelphia: Lippincott, 1973), p. 219.

4. Plant, p. 212.

5. Ibid., p. 7.

6. Quoted in Ben S. Austin, "Homosexuals and the Holocaust," n.d., <http://www.mtsu.edu/~baustin/homobg.html> (March 15, 2001).

7. Michael Burleigh and Wolfgang Wipperman, *The Racial State: Germany, 1933–1945* (New York: Cambridge University Press, 1991), p. 192.

8. David W. Dunlap, "Personalizing Nazis' Homosexual Victims," <http://www. english. upenn.edu/~afilreis/Holocaust/personalize-gays. htms> (March 15, 2001).

9. Heinz Heger, *The Men With the Pink Triangle* (Boston: Alyson Publishing Co., 1980), p. 37.

10. Plant, p. 181.

11. Robert N. Proctor, *Racial Hygiene: Medicine Under the Nazis* (Boston: Harvard University Press, 1988), p. 122.

12. Ibid., p. 133.

Glossary

Aryan—Nazi term for Nordic, or Northern European, peoples.

atrocity—A brutal or horrifying act.

communism—A form of government in which property is communally owned.

decree—A formal and authoritative order.

eugenics—Improving a race or breed by controlling mating.

euthanasia—Mercy killing; in Nazi Germany, the practice of killing handicapped individuals who were considered useless.

gene—The biological unit of heredity.

genetics—The science dealing with inherited characteristics of life-forms.

Gestapo *(Geheime-Staats-Polizei)*—A secret state police agency in Nazi Germany.

hereditary—Capable of being passed from one generation to another.

homophobic—Hatred and fear of homosexuals.

homosexuality—Sexual activity between members of the same sex.

lebensraum—Living space; Nazi term for expansion of German territory.

master race—Nazi term for Germanic peoples who were regarded as superior to all other races.

non-aggression pact—An agreement between two governments, pledging not to attack one another.

parasite—A creature that lives off another, without returning anything of value.

proletariat—The working class, who sell their labor for wages.

propaganda—A presentation of ideas slanted to shape and control public opinion.

racial hygiene—The idea of protecting the genetic health of a people through selective breeding and other measures.

racism—An irrational belief in the superiority of a given group, based upon inborn racial traits.

SA (*Sturmabteilung*)—Storm troops; in the early days of the Nazi party, a private army used to intimidate and control enemies. Often called "Brownshirts" after the color of their uniforms.

SS (*Schutzstaffel*)—Protection squad; the elite guard of the Nazi state. It administered the Final Solution and insured obedience to the dictates of the Führer.

Slavic—A language and ethnic grouping which includes Russians, Ukrainians, Poles, and other eastern Europeans.

sterilize—To deprive of the ability to produce offspring.

subhuman—Less than human; an individual possessing many animal-like qualities.

warrant—A legal order permitting arrest, search, or seizure of property.

wild euthanasia—Killing of handicapped persons without legal authorization.

Further Reading

Ayer, Eleanor H., Helen Waterford, and Alfons Heck. *Parallel Journeys*. New York: Aladdin Paperbacks, 2000.

Dvorson, Alexa. *Hitler Youth: Marching Toward Madness*. New York: Rosen Publishing Group, 1998.

Friedman, Ina R. *The Other Victims: First-Person Stories of Non-Jews Persecuted by the Nazis*. New York: Houghton Mifflin Co., 1990.

Marrin, Albert. *Hitler*. New York: Penguin Putnam Books for Young Readers, 1993.

Sharp, Anne Wallace. *The Gypsies*. San Diego: Lucent Books, 2002.

Vogel, Ilse-Margret. *Bad Times, Good Friends: A Memoir—Berlin 1945*. San Diego: Harcourt Brace Jovanovich, 1992.

Internet Addresses

Simon Wiesenthal Center: Multimedia Learning Center
http://motlc.wiesenthal.org/index.html

United States Holocaust Memorial Museum
http://www.ushmm.org

Index

A

abortion, 12, 80, 85–86, 89

Aryan, 11, 14, 25, 41, 45, 51, 75, 89

B

Birkenau, 70–71

Brandt, Karl, 19, 21

Britain, 30–32

C

Chelmno extermination camp, 69

commissars, 46

communism, 43, 44, 51

Communists, 28, 45, 46

concentration camps, 30, 35, 36, 39, 41, 62, 64, 66, 67, 81, 85

D

dehumanize, 49

Deuschl, Hans, 53

E

Eastern Europe, 28, 51

Eichmann, Adolf, 67

Einsatzgruppen, 49, 69, 70

eugenics, 17

euthanasia, 12, 18–19, 21, 23–25

F

forced sterilization, 12, 16–18, 39

G

gadje, 57, 59–60

Galton, Francis, 17

Garstka, Dr. Stanley M., 36, 37, 39

genes, 16

genetic health court, 88

German youth, 11

Gestapo, 78, 80

Gypsies, 14, 57, 59–61, 62, 64, 65, 66, 67, 69, 70, 71, 73–74

Gypsy project, 60

H

heredity, 16, 17

Himmler, Heinrich, 53, 62, 64–65, 66, 70, 79–81

Hitler, Adolf, 7, 11, 14, 17, 18–19, 21, 23, 27, 28, 30, 31, 32, 34–35, 41, 43, 44, 45–47, 49, 51, 54–56, 60, 76, 78

Hitler-Stalin pact, 28, 45

homosexuals, 12, 75, 76, 78, 79, 80, 81, 83

I

interracial marriage, 85

J

Jagiellonian University, 35

K

Kracow, Poland, 35

L

labor camps, 39

Law for the Prevention of Genetically Diseased Offspring, 18

lebensraum, 32

Lenin, Vladimir Illyich, 43

Lithuania, 30

Lodz ghetto, 67, 69

Luftwaffe, 47, 48

lungo drom, 57, 74

M

Marital Health Law, 88

Marx, Karl, 43

master race, 11, 45

medicalized murder, 25

Mengele, Josef, 71, 73, 74

mental illness, 12, 22

mental retardation, 12, 21–22

Minsk, 48

Mischlinge, 61

Moscow, Russia, 54

N

Neuengamme concentration camp, 39

newborn babies, reporting of handicapped, 21

Nuremberg Laws, 88

O

Operation Barbarossa, 45, 46

P

Paragraph 175, 79, 81, 83, 85

Pawiak prison, 36, 39

Poland, 27–28, 30, 32, 41

Poles, 14, 27, 28, 31, 32, 34, 35, 36–37, 39, 41

Porraimos, 67, 73

POW, 52, 53

R

race, 14, 15, 28

race criminals, 12, 75

racial health, 12

racial hygiene, 15, 85

racism, 16, 25

Ritter, Robert, 60

Röhm, Ernst, 76

Russia, 43, 44, 45, 46, 47, 49, 51, 54, 56

Russians, 28, 43, 46, 47, 48, 49, 51–52, 53, 55, 69

S

SA (Stormtroops), 76, 78

Sachsenhausen concen-
tration camp, 66, 83

Slavic peoples, 14, 28

social classes, 45

Soviet Union, 28, 32, 46,
47, 51

SS, 27, 30, 35, 53, 62, 69,
73, 78, 79

Stalin, Josef, 28, 43,
45–47

Stalingrad, 56

Stormtroops, 76

T

T4 program, 22, 23

U

Ukrainians, 28, 49

Union of Soviet Socialist
Republics (USSR),
30, 44

United States, 51

V

Volk (German people),
18, 25

W

Warsaw University, 36

wild euthanasia, 23, 25

World War II, 27